Working Together

a Turkish restaurant

Gary Underwood

Australian Multicultural Foundation

Blake
EDUCATION
Better ways to learn

Acknowledgments

We would like to thank the Ademoglu family, Ala Turc'A Café Restaurant, for their contribution and participation.

Working Together: a Turkish restaurant

ISBN: 1 74164 096 2

Written by Gary Underwood
Copyright © 2006 Blake Publishing
Published by Blake Education Pty Ltd
ABN 50 074 266 023
108 Main Rd
Clayton South VIC 3168
Ph: (03) 9558 4433
Fax: (03) 9558 5433
email: mail@blake.com.au
Visit our website: www.blake.com.au

Harmony and Understanding program developed by UC Publishing Pty Ltd
Designer: Luke Sharrock
Series Editor: Hass Dellal
Editor: Kerry Nagle

Printed in Malaysia by Thumbprints Utd Sdn Bhd

Photo and illustration credits:
MAPgraphics, page 7.
All other photographs and illustrations are © copyright UC Publishing Pty Ltd.
Every effort has been made to trace the holders of copyrighted photographs. If any omission can be rectified, the publishers will be pleased to make the necessary arrangements.

Contents

In this book …

Introduction

Altan and Sevim own their own restaurant called Ala Turc'A Café Restaurant. They have three daughters – Gülcan, Gülsen and Sibel.

Gülcan is the eldest and she is away at university. Gülsen and Sibel go to school, but at weekends they help their parents in the restaurant.

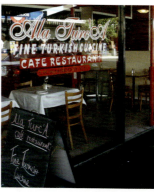

Turkish heritage

Altan and Sevim left Turkey to start a new life for themselves and their daughters.

The family is very proud of being part of their new country. But Altan and Sevim also teach their girls Turkish recipes, songs and dances so they will know something of their Turkish heritage and culture.

Fast fact

Many Turkish people have migrated from Turkey and set up homes in other countries. There are now large Turkish communities living all over the world.

Country facts: Turkey

- Turkey has a unique geographical location, lying partly in Europe and partly in Asia, just north of the Middle East.

- It is bound on the north by the Black Sea and on the south by the Mediterranean Sea. It has borders with Iran, Iraq, Syria, Georgia, Armenia, Greece and Bulgaria.

- Turkey has a population of 68 million people.

- Its capital city is Ankara.

- Its largest city is Istanbul.

- The main religion of Turkey is Islam.

Working in the restaurant

The family spends a lot of time together, working in the restaurant. They all have their special jobs to do.

Altan is the chef and in charge of the kitchen. He cooks traditional Turkish foods.

Sevim, the mother of the family, manages the reservations and seating. She also looks after the cash register and the finances of the business.

Turkish food

There are many different types of Turkish food.

Turkish food is famous around the world. The food includes such dishes as pilav, a rice dish; kebabs, which are grilled or roasted meat usually on skewers; börek, a pastry filled with meat, cheese and potatoes; and the famous Turkish bread, pide.

Fast fact

During the Ottoman Empire, the Sultan's palace kitchen was a place of great importance. Hundreds of cooks specialising in different types of dishes fed as many as ten thousand people a day. Many regions throughout the empire adopted Turkish cuisine.

Preparing for customers

Every day before the restaurant opens, Gülsen and Sibel sweep the floors and wipe over the tables and chairs.

They set each table with a tablecloth, napkins, plates, cutlery and glasses.

Why is cleanliness important?

It is very important to keep restaurants clean. Because they feed so many people, restaurants must make sure that the cooking and eating areas are free from pests and unhealthy germs.

The nargile

Sibel's most important job is dusting the nargile.

The nargile is used traditionally as a water-pipe, but in the restaurant it's only used for decoration. This nargile has been in Altan's family for many generations. His father brought it from Turkey when he migrated to live in his new country.

Fast fact

The nargile was a traditional pipe that became popular during the Ottoman Empire. The pipe was used for smoking tobacco and the men would sit in groups, talking and inhaling long, deep breaths of smoke.

Turkish decorations

The family have other traditional Turkish ornaments and special plates that decorate the restaurant.

This way, Altan and his family can share some traditional Turkish art and culture, as well as food, with their customers.

Fast fact

Turkish art was very popular during the days of the Ottoman Empire and still is today. Turkish rugs and pottery, with their fascinating geometric patterns, are very popular.

The family dinner

Altan prepares all the food for the restaurant customers, but Gülsen and Sibel take turns to help him prepare their own evening meal, which they eat before the restaurant opens.

One of their favourite meals is a mezze platter, followed by kebabs.

Turkish meals often start off with a mezze platter as an appetiser. The platter is usually served with vegetables, pasta and fish.

Making the mezze platter

Sibel helps her father make the mezze platter. It has all sorts of different vegetables and dips such as eggplant, chickpea and yoghurt on a bed of lettuce leaves.

Salad vegetables are then added along with grilled eggplant, capsicum and zucchini.

Word fact

The word "yoghurt" comes from the Turkish word *yogurtmak* meaning "to blend". This refers to how yoghurt is made – the "blending" of bacteria with milk to begin the fermentation process.

The mezze platter is finished off with some octopus and rice wrapped in vine leaves. These are called dolmas.

Sprigs of parsley are put on the platter. A special dressing is drizzled over it all.

The mezze platter is ready to eat!

Making kebabs

Kebabs are a famous Turkish traditional food.

The family loves to eat kofte kebabs. These are spicy minced lamb wrapped around large, flat skewers.

Fast fact

Shish kebab, which in Turkish means "skewer" and "grilled meat", is a famous Turkish meal. Kebabs were originally a dish of nomadic tribes. The marinade not only tenderised wild game, but added flavour. The skewers were a common cooking solution for tribes who didn't have the benefit of ovens and stove tops.

The kebabs are placed on the hot grill.

It is very hot. The meat starts to sizzle as soon as it is put on the hotplate. The girls are keen to learn how to cook, but Altan always keeps a watchful eye on his daughters when they use the hot grill.

Burn treatment

Cooking can be a lot of fun but you have to be careful when using grills, hotplates or barbecues. Always make sure you are with an adult. But if you do get a burn, remember to:

- apply cold water to the burn for at least five minutes

- never puncture any blisters which may occur

- always see a doctor if the burn is serious.

Turkish delight

After eating the main meal, the family enjoys a favourite dessert, Turkish delight.

A toothpick is placed in each piece so people will not get all sticky when they pick it up.

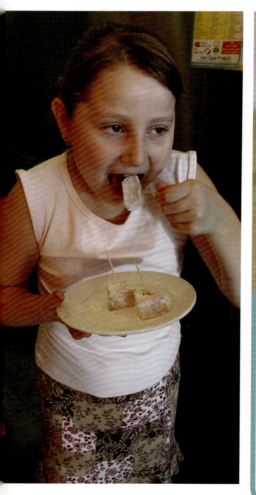

Fast fact

Turkish delight is called *lokum* in Turkey. It is like a stiff, sweet jelly that has been rolled in icing sugar. Turkish delight is popular all around the world.

Turkish coffee

At the end of the meal, Sevim makes some Turkish coffee for herself and Altan.

Fast fact

Coffee was first discovered in Ethiopia, where tribes would eat the bean because it gave them energy.

Coffee was first made into a drink in Turkey, where it was usually drunk with herbs for extra flavour.

Today, coffee is a very popular drink all over the world.

Time to relax

The family dinner is always early, before the customers come.

Once they arrive, it is so busy that there is little time to talk and relax. The family welcomes this time to sit together before the real work starts.

Work is over

Turkish food is good to eat. But living and working in a Turkish restaurant can be hard work.

There's always heaps of cleaning to do and dishes to wash at the end of the night.

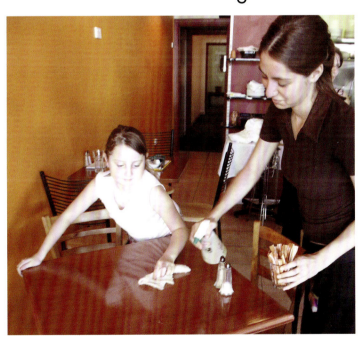 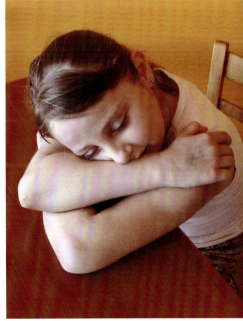

The Turkish way

For centuries, the Turkish people have been a people of friendly hospitality who love to share their amazing food.

When Turkish people move to new countries to live, they take with them the recipes and customs. Not only does it help them remember their culture, it is something they can share with others.

Glossary

börek   Turkish pastry filled with meat or vegetables

culture   the art, ideas and way of life of a group of people

custom   something that a group of people usually does

hospitality   being friendly to guests and looking after them well

kebab   grilled or roasted meat

mezze   Turkish appetisers

migrate   leave your country to go and live in another country

nargile   Turkish water pipe, traditionally used for smoking

Ottoman Empire
              Turkish empire that was very powerful from the 16th to the 19th century

pide   flat, oval Turkish bread

pilav   Turkish rice dish

Index